DISCOVERING PLANETS

Nicolas Brasch

Australia • Brazil • Japan • Korea • Mexico • Singapore • Spain • United Kingdom • United States

Discovering Planets

Fast Forward
Blue Level 9

Text: Nicolas Brasch
Editor: Kate McGough
Design: Vonda Pestana
Series design: James Lowe
Production controller: Emma Hayes
Photo research: Gillian Cardinal
Audio recordings: Juliet Hill, Picture Start
Spoken by: Matthew King and Abbe Holmes
Reprint: Siew Han Ong

Acknowledgements
The author and publisher would like to acknowledge permission to reproduce material from the following sources:
Photographs by AAP Images, p 13; Akg-images, p 11; photolibrary.com/SPL, cover, pp 1, 3, 4-5, 6, 7, 8, 9, 10, 12, 14, 15.

ISBN 978 0 17 012535 2
ISBN 978 0 17 012525 3 (set)

Cengage Learning Australia
Level 7, 80 Dorcas Street
South Melbourne, Victoria Australia 3205
Phone: 1300 790 853

Cengage Learning New Zealand
Unit 4B Rosedale Office Park
331 Rosedale Road, Albany, North Shore NZ 0632
Phone: 0800 449 725

For learning solutions, visit **cengage.com.au**

Printed in China by 1010 Printing International Ltd
7 8 9 10 16 15

Evaluated in independent research by staff from the Department of Language, Literacy and Arts Education at the University of Melbourne.

DISCOVERING PLANETS

Nicolas Brasch

Contents

Chapter 1

THE SOLAR SYSTEM

The Solar System is made up of the Sun, planets and other bodies, like comets.

The Sun is a star.
It is in the middle of the Solar System.
The planets move around the Sun.

There are nine planets.
People **discovered** these nine planets over a very long time.

There were no **telescopes**
thousands of years ago.
People could see five planets
in the sky without the use of telescopes.

These five planets were:

These five planets and Earth are the six planets closest to the Sun.

There are another three planets that cannot be seen without the use of telescopes.
They are:

Pluto
(dwarf
planet)

Chapter 2

DISCOVERING URANUS

THE NEWS OF THE DAY

13 March, 1781

An **astronomer** has just made an important discovery. He has discovered a new planet. This planet has been named Uranus, and is said to be the furthest planet from the Sun.

The astronomer said, "I am very happy to have discovered this new planet. There could be other planets out there that we have not seen yet."

William Herschel discovered Uranus.

Chapter 3

DISCOVERING NEPTUNE

The News of the Day

23 September, 1846

A new planet has been discovered.
An astronomer saw the new planet
with his telescope.
This planet has been named Neptune,
and is said to be the furthest planet
from the Sun.

The astronomer said,
"This is the best day of my life.
I have worked very hard
and now I have discovered
a new planet.
I am very happy."

Johann Galle discovered Neptune.

Chapter 4

DISCOVERING PLUTO

THE NEWS OF THE DAY

23 January, 1930

We have a new planet.
It is called Pluto.
An astronomer discovered Pluto today.
It is said to be the furthest planet
from the Sun.

The astronomer said,
"It is hard to believe
that this planet has been out there
for so long, and we have not
seen it before now."

"That shows just how big the Solar System is.
There may be other planets out there
that have not been discovered."

Clyde Tombaugh discovered Pluto.

Chapter 5

DISCOVERING MORE PLANETS

an astronomer using a strong telescope

Sometimes, astronomers look for a new planet after seeing other planets move in strange ways. They may move in these strange ways because another planet is close by.

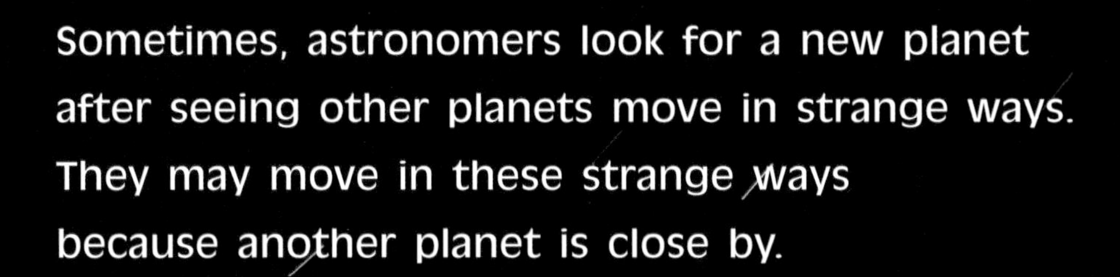

Stronger telescopes are being made all the time. This means that other planets in the Solar System may be discovered using these new telescopes.

Glossary

astronomer a person who studies space and all the things in it

discovered found out about

telescopes instruments used to see up close things that are very far away

Index